BRIDGE

to Open Seas

JN081144

BUN-EIDO

CONTENTS

Let's Read ABCs

Let's Write ABCs

Let's Talk

Do You Know This?

Let's Say It

❶ CONSONANTS 1-3 ———— 30

❷ VOWELS 1-3 ———— 33

COUNTRIES OF THE WORLD ———— 36

List of Words & Phrases ———— 38

大文字ではじまる語句 39

DAYS / MONTHS / 略語・短縮形 / A-Y

カテゴリー別リスト 40

1. 動作
2. 状態・気持ち
3. 飲食物
4. 数
5. 学校生活
6. 町・施設・職業
7. 日常生活
8. スポーツ
9. 色・形
10. 季節・時間
11. 国・都市
12. 動植物
13. 自然・天気
14. 祝祭日・趣味・遊び
15. 人と身体
16. その他（抽象語）
17. その他（ことば）
18. 主な連語

ABC 順リスト 52

大文字ではじまる語句およびカテゴリー別リストにある語句

和英リスト 62

動詞・形容詞・名詞

▶ **音声トラック番号：** 1 〜 71

1 〜 5 *pp. 4 - 5* **LISTEN & READ ALOUD**

6 〜 11 *pp. 18-20* **Let's Talk**

12 〜 33 *pp. 21-28* **Do You Know This?**

34 〜 71 *pp. 30-35* **Let's Say It**

1 LISTEN & READ ALOUD 1: a-m

Aa
ant
alarm
astronaut
apple
artist

Bb
boy
baby
bird
bicycle
bridge

Cc
car
clock
cherry
computer
circle

Dd
dog
doll
desk
dinosaur
dragonfly

Ee
egg
eye
elephant
eraser
eight

Ff
fish
face
flower
fireworks
fox

Gg
girl
glove
guitar
gorilla
grasshopper

Hh
hamburger
head
heart
horse
house

Ii
ink
ice cream
I
island
idea

Jj
jam
juice
Japan
jet
judo

Kk
kite
king
kiwi
knife
knee

Ll
lemon
light
lettuce
leg
lion

Mm
math
mother
mushroom
mouse
mouth

❷ LISTEN & READ ALOUD 2: n-z

②

Nn nest
nose
nurse
notebook
newspaper

Oo orange
oil
onion
owl
Olympics

Pp peach
phone
popcorn
pencil
piano

Qq quiz
quiet
queen
question
quit

Rr ring
road
ruler
recorder
rabbit

Ss sun
snow
scissors
star
square

Tt train
television
table
tiger
triangle

Uu umbrella
uniform
unicycle
UFO
uncle

Vv violin
vacation
five
vet
vase

Ww wall
watch
wheelchair
watermelon
welcome

Xx box
exit
taxi
textbook
six

Yy yo-yo
yacht
yes
yen
YouTube

Zz zoo
zipper
zero
zebra
pizza

"**Spelling Bee**" 英単語のスペリングを正確に言うゲーム形式の練習です. ③ a-m ④ n-z ⑤ a-z
説明をよく聞いて，楽しみながらやってみましょう.

❶ BLOCK LETTERS: CAPITAL LETTERS
大文字のブロック体

ABCDEFGHIJKLMNOPQRSTUVWXYZ

●基本ストローク（筆の運び方）

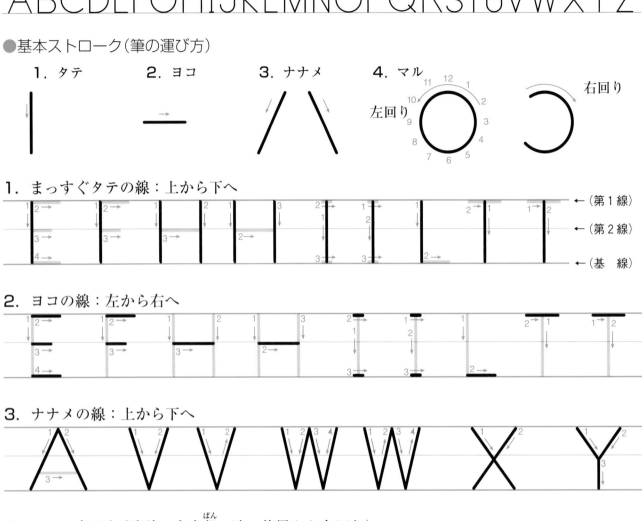

1. まっすぐタテの線：上から下へ

← （第１線）
← （第２線）
← （基　線）

2. ヨコの線：左から右へ

3. ナナメの線：上から下へ

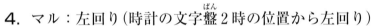

4. マル：左回り（時計の文字盤２時の位置から左回り）

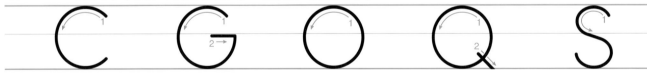

5. タテ／ヨコとナナメの組合わせ

6. タテとマルの組合わせ

※**注意**　原則としてタテを優先し，ヨコはあとから書きます．（漢字とは異なります）
　　　　　大文字の高さは，すべて第１線と基線の幅と同じになります．

SMALL LETTERS
小文字のブロック体

● 文字の大きさ（高さ）による区分

abcdefghijklmnopqrstuvwxyz

← （第1線）
← （第2線）
← （基　線）
← （第4線）

acemnorsuvwxz　bdfhkl　gpqy　ijt

1. タテ／ヨコ／ナナメの線

k l v v v w w x y z

2. タテとうね（hill）の線

h m n r

3. マルとタテ／ヨコの線

a b c d e g o p q s u

4. 短い横棒線を引く

f t t

5. テンを打つ

i j

● 大文字と同じ筆順で，大きさ（高さ）がちがうブロック体

Cc Kk Oo Pp Ss

Vv Vv Ww Ww Xx Zz

7

Let's Write ABCs

❷ CONFUSING LETTERS 形が似ているアルファベット

●形が似ている大文字の練習

CGO

OQ

EFLT

IJLH

PRB

UV

BDO

MNH

●形が似ている小文字の練習
b, d, p, q の筆順に注意：タテの長い線の左部分は先に，右部分はあとに書きます．
d, q → 左部分を先に書いてからタテ線
b, p → タテ線を先に書いてから右部分

a d   b d

c e   c o

i j   g q

f t   m n

v y   p q

v w   n r

h n   n u

u v   d p   q b

Let's Write ABCs

❸ **WRITE: a-j**   **1** 5回ずつ書いてみましょう. **2** 下の2行に1〜10を2回ずつ書いてみましょう.

1. apple

2. bridge

3. cherry

4. desk

5. eraser

6. face

7. guitar

8. heart

9. idea

10. juice

Let's Write ABCs

❹ **WRITE: k-t** **1** 5回ずつ書いてみましょう. **2** 下の2行に**1～10**を2回ずつ書いてみましょう.

1. knife

2. light

3. mother

4. nurse

5. orange

6. pencil

7. quiet

8. ruler

9. square

10. table

Let's Write ABCs

❺ WRITE: u-z 　**1** 5回ずつ書いてみましょう. **2** 下の2行に**1～10**を2回ずつ書いてみましょう.

1. umbrella

2. violin

3. watch

4. exit

5. yo-yo

6. zipper

7. Japan

8. ATM

9. UFO

10. Olympics

Let's Write ABCs

❻ EXERCISE

1 Put them into ALPHABETICAL ORDER. ABC 順になるように番号をつけなさい.

（例）	①	②	③	④
how (3)	wax ( )	toy ( )	bay ( )	sea ( )
cow (2)	tax ( )	soy ( )	may ( )	pea ( )
bow (1)	max ( )	boy ( )	say ( )	tea ( )

⑤	⑥	⑦	⑧	⑨
bag ( )	cat ( )	the ( )	map ( )	yen ( )
are ( )	ten ( )	eve ( )	pan ( )	net ( )
get ( )	ant ( )	hot ( )	act ( )	eat ( )

⑩	⑪	⑫	⑬	⑭
NGO ( )	MLB ( )	COD ( )	KIX ( )	RSVP ( )
FAQ ( )	NBA ( )	ATM ( )	HND ( )	BYOD ( )
GPS ( )	MBA ( )	IOU ( )	NRT ( )	ASAP ( )

⑮	⑯	⑰	⑱
cat ( )	girl ( )	skirt ( )	blue ( )
car ( )	game ( )	shirt ( )	black ( )
cap ( )	green ( )	shoes ( )	brown ( )
cup ( )	gold ( )	socks ( )	beige ( )
card ( )	guitar ( )	shorts ( )	bronze ( )

2 Put the letters in ALPHABETICAL ORDER. 例にならって，アルファベットを ABC 順に並べかえ，単語を完成しなさい.

（例）n a t   ant

1. x o b _____
2. y b o _____
3. s o t m _____

4. p o y c _____
5. w n k o _____
6. i y c t _____

7. l t b e _____
8. f m l i _____
9. i n b g e _____

3 Put the words in ALPHABETICAL ORDER. 単語を ABC 順に並べかえ，英文を完成しなさい.

July   Ayame's   is   birthday   tenth   .

_____

play   he   volleyball   Can   well   ?

_____

4 先生の指示にしたがって，ブロック体の練習をしましょう．

1.

2.

3.

4.

5.

6.

7.

8.

9.

10.

11.

12.

Let's Talk

❶ GREETINGS あいさつ

⑥ **1** **Talk with your friends.**

(1) A : My name is _____ . Nice to meet you.

B : Hello. I'm _____ . Nice to meet you, too.

(2) A : Hello. I'm _____ . I'm a junior high school student.

I'm from _____ .

B : Hi. My name is _____ . I'm a junior high school student,

too. I'm from _____ . But I live in _____ now.

(3) A : How are you?

B : Good, thank you. And you?

A : Pretty good, thanks.

2 **Write your greetings.**

_____

_____

3 **Write the 10 place names.**

Chiba

Fukuoka

Hiroshima

Kyoto

Nara

Osaka

Sapporo

Tokyo

Yokohama

Mt. Fuji

❷ LIKES & DISLIKES 好き嫌い

1 Talk with your friends. ⑦

(1) A: I like dogs. How about you?

　　B: I don't like dogs, but I like cats. Do you like cats?

　　A: Yes, I do.

(2) A: I like ramen. How about you?

　　B: I don't like ramen, but I like udon. Do you like udon?

　　A: No, I don't.

(3) A: I like soccer. How about you?

　　B: I like soccer, too!

　　A: Really? Let's play together!

2 Talk with your friends. **Toolbox** から語(句)を選び，ペアで話してみましょう. ⑧

A: I like ＿＿＿＿＿. How about you?

B: I don't like ＿＿＿＿, but I like ＿＿＿＿. Do you like ＿＿＿＿?

A: Yes, I do. / No, I don't.

Toolbox 1

snakes　　spiders　　bees　　mice　　horses　　deer　　bears　　monkeys ⑨

Toolbox 2

cheese　　tomatoes　　mushrooms　　eggplants　　watermelon　　onions
carrots　　cucumbers　　grapes　　okonomiyaki　　pizza　　rice　　natto

Toolbox 3

baseball　　volleyball　　tennis　　table tennis　　handball　　basketball
judo　　sumo　　rugby　　swimming　　skiing　　badminton

Let's Talk

❸ GETTING TO KNOW EACH OTHER　お互いを知る

⑩　**1** Talk with your friends.

(1) A: I play baseball.　Can you play baseball?

　　B: Yes, I can.

(2) A: I play the piano.　Can you play the piano?

　　B: No, I can't.

(3) A: How old are you?

　　B: I'm thirteen.　What about you?

(4) A: When is your birthday?

　　B: My birthday is October 1st.　How about you?

　　A: My birthday is November 23rd.

(5) A: Happy birthday, ＿＿＿＿＿＿＿.　This is for you.

　　B: Oh, thank you, ＿＿＿＿＿＿＿.

　　A: You're welcome.

⑪　**2** Talk with your friends. **Toolbox**から語(句)を選び，ペアで話してみましょう.

A: I want to be (a・an) ＿＿＿＿＿＿＿.　How about you?

B: I want to be (a・an) ＿＿＿＿＿＿＿.

Toolbox

doctor	nurse		police officer	designer
engineer	teacher		train conductor	baseball player
artist	musician	singer	game creator	*YouTuber

*YouTuber ユーチューバー

20

❶ CLASSROOM ENGLISH　教室で使う英語

● Teacher　　　　　　　　　　　　　　　　　● Student(s)

1
| Good morning,
Good afternoon, | everybody.
class.
boys and girls. |

➡

⑫
| Good morning,
Good afternoon, | Ms. Kimura.
Mr. King. |

2
| Let's see who is absent (today). | Nanami?
Jon?
Yumi?
Rikuya? |

➡

⑬
Yes. Here. Present.
[He / She] is absent. [He / She] is not here today.

3

⑭
| OK!
Be quiet, please.
Right!
All right! | Let's begin today's lesson.
I think we can start now. | Open your textbook to page xx.
Close your textbook.
Look at the [blackboard/whiteboard].
[Open/Close] your computer.
Turn [on/off] your [computer/tablet]. |

4
| Listen to me.
Repeat after me.
Raise your hand.
Any questions? |

5

⑮
| Can you speak more slowly?
Can you repeat that?
Can you say that again?
I have a question. What does "XXX" mean? |

6
| For your homework, do Exercises 1 to 4.
Before the next class, finish Exercise 5.
At home, learn how to spell these words.
　　　　learn the conversation on page 14. |

⑯
| Please give me the homework now.
Please collect the homework.
Please pass these out. |

7

⑰
| [Very] good.
Well done.
Good job. | That's all for today. Goodbye. |
| | See you | tomorrow.
Friday.
next week. |

➡
| Goodbye, | Ms. Kimura.
Mr. King. |

❷ FAMILY TREE 家系図

⑱

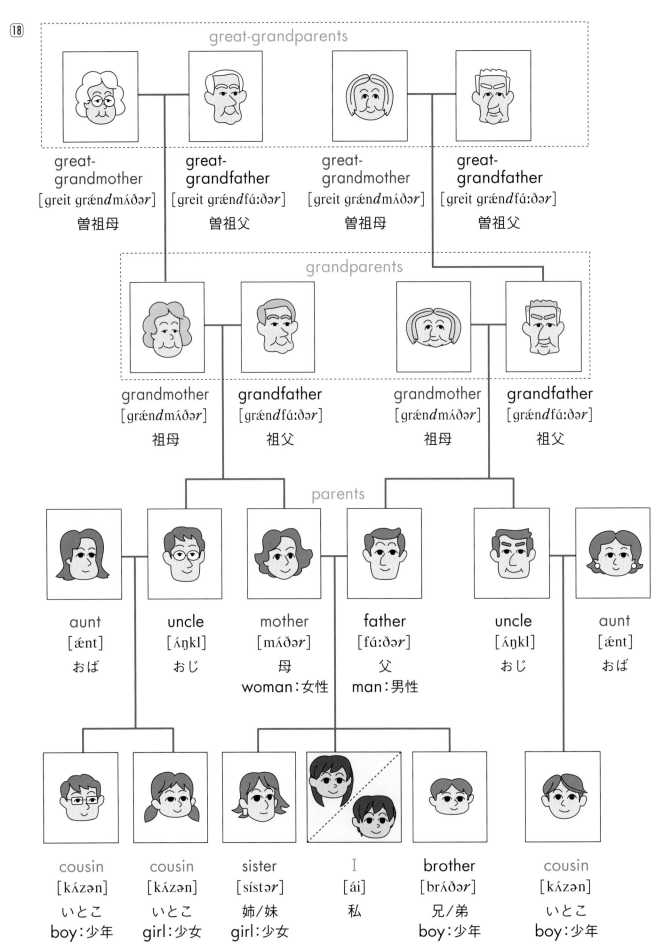

great-grandparents

great-grandmother
[greit grǽndmʌ́ðər]
曽祖母

great-grandfather
[greit grǽndfɑ́:ðər]
曽祖父

great-grandmother
[greit grǽndmʌ́ðər]
曽祖母

great-grandfather
[greit grǽndfɑ́:ðər]
曽祖父

grandparents

grandmother
[grǽndmʌ́ðər]
祖母

grandfather
[grǽndfɑ́:ðər]
祖父

grandmother
[grǽndmʌ́ðər]
祖母

grandfather
[grǽndfɑ́:ðər]
祖父

parents

aunt
[ǽnt]
おば

uncle
[ʌ́ŋkl]
おじ

mother
[mʌ́ðər]
母
woman：女性

father
[fɑ́:ðər]
父
man：男性

uncle
[ʌ́ŋkl]
おじ

aunt
[ǽnt]
おば

cousin
[kʌ́zən]
いとこ
boy：少年

cousin
[kʌ́zən]
いとこ
girl：少女

sister
[sístər]
姉/妹
girl：少女

I
[ái]
私

brother
[brʌ́ðər]
兄/弟
boy：少年

cousin
[kʌ́zən]
いとこ
boy：少年

❸ COLORS 色　See, see see!　What colors do I see?

⑲

Pink grapefruits,

Purple plums and eggplants,

Green cucumbers,

Red apples and tomatoes,

Blueberries are blue,

And oranges are orange.

Brown chestnuts,

Yellow bananas and lemons,

White rice and brown rice,

White wine and red wine.

But black coffee isn't really black, is it?

⑳　■ MEDALS　メダル

silver　gold　bronze

㉑　■ RAINBOW　虹

Red
Orange
Yellow
Green
Blue
Indigo
Violet
└ Roy G. Biv

㉒　■ TRAFFIC LIGHT　交通信号
red, yellow, green

㉓ ❹ **PARTS OF THE BODY** 体の部分

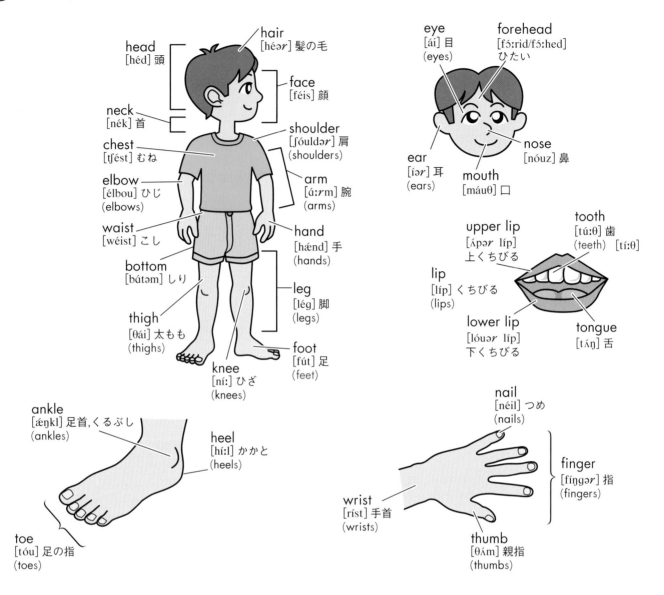

head [héd] 頭
hair [héər] 髪の毛
face [féis] 顔
neck [nék] 首
shoulder [ʃóuldər] 肩 (shoulders)
chest [tʃést] むね
arm [á:rm] 腕 (arms)
elbow [élbou] ひじ (elbows)
waist [wéist] こし
hand [hǽnd] 手 (hands)
bottom [bátəm] しり
leg [lég] 脚 (legs)
thigh [θái] 太もも (thighs)
foot [fút] 足 (feet)
knee [ní:] ひざ (knees)

eye [ái] 目 (eyes)
forehead [fɔ́:rid/fɔ́:hed] ひたい
ear [íər] 耳 (ears)
nose [nóuz] 鼻
mouth [máuθ] 口

upper lip [ʌ́pər líp] 上くちびる
tooth [tú:θ] 歯 (teeth) [tí:θ]
lip [líp] くちびる (lips)
lower lip [lóuər líp] 下くちびる
tongue [tʌ́ŋ] 舌

ankle [ǽŋkl] 足首,くるぶし (ankles)
heel [hí:l] かかと (heels)
toe [tóu] 足の指 (toes)

nail [néil] つめ (nails)
finger [fíŋgər] 指 (fingers)
wrist [ríst] 手首 (wrists)
thumb [θʌ́m] 親指 (thumbs)

㉔ **Let's play SIMON SAYS** ゲーム

SAYS [séz] の発音に注意

① Simon 役を1人選ぶ.
② Simon は,ゲーム参加者に英語で「命令」を出す.
③ ゲーム参加者は,Simon の英語を聞き,すばやく反応する.
　a) Simon says, "...!" と言ってから出された命令には従わなければならない.
　b) Simon says, "...!" とは言われずに出された命令には従ってはいけない.
④ Simon says, "...!" と言われたとき,命令と異なる動作をしたり,Simon says, "...!" と言われていないときに間違って命令に従った者はその時点でゲームから外れる.
⑤ 最後まで残った人が「勝者」で,次の Simon 役をする.

■ ゲームで使う命令と動作

Stand up. (On your feet.) →立ち上がる
Sit down. →すわる
Touch your 〜. →自分の〜に触る
Point at your 〜. →自分の〜を指さす
Raise your (right / left) hand. →(右/左)手をあげる

Close your eyes. →目を閉じる
Open your mouth. →口をあける
Play baseball. →野球(のまね)をする
Play the piano. →ピアノを弾く(まねをする)

❺ EXERCISE　次の各グループ(A～F)の単語をそれぞれ ABC 順になるよう並べかえ，下線部につづりを記入しなさい．A. FAMILY は，答えの一部が書いてあります．

4 Put them into ALPHABETICAL ORDER.

A. FAMILY	B. COLORS	C. BODY	D. ANIMALS	E. FOOD	F. SPORTS
cousin	red	knee	snakes	tomatoes	soccer
brother	white	eye	spiders	cheese	volleyball
grandmother	yellow	ear	birds	kiwis	baseball
aunt	purple	arm	monkeys	mushrooms	tennis

A. FAMILY	B. COLORS	C. BODY
aunt		
brother		

D. ANIMALS	E. FOOD	F. SPORTS

❻ DAYS OF THE WEEK & MONTHS 曜日・月

㉕ ■ DAYS OF THE WEEK

Monday 月曜日
Tuesday 火曜日
Wednesday 水曜日
Thursday 木曜日
Friday 金曜日
Saturday 土曜日
Sunday 日曜日

㉖

Monday's child has a pretty face,	月曜生まれの子どもは器量よし
Tuesday's child loves to race,	火曜生まれの子どもはかけっこ大好き
Wednesday's child has a kind heart,	水曜生まれの子どもは心優しく
Thursday's child is very smart,	木曜生まれの子どもはとってもお利口
Friday's child likes singing and dancing,	金曜生まれの子どもは歌と踊りがお気に入り
Saturday's child works hard for a living,	土曜生まれの子どもは働き者で
Sunday's child is loving and giving.	日曜生まれの子どもは愛情豊か

（nursery rhyme 童謡）

㉗ ■ MONTHS

1月 Snow in January. 1月は雪	2月 Ice in February. 2月は氷	3月 Wind in March. 3月は風
4月 Rain in April. 4月は雨	5月 Buds in May. 5月は芽	6月 Roses in June. 6月はバラ
7月 Play in July. 7月は遊び	8月 Hot days in August. 8月は暑い日	9月 School in September. 9月は学校
10月 Apples in October. 10月はリンゴ	11月 Cold days in November. 11月は寒い日	12月 Christmas in December. 12月はクリスマス

❼ SEASONS & WEATHER 季節・天候

㉘ ■ SEASONS

spring

summer

autumn（fall）

winter

■ TEMPERATURE 気温 ㉛

What's the temperature now?
— It's 30 degrees Celsius.
— It's 86 degrees Fahrenheit.

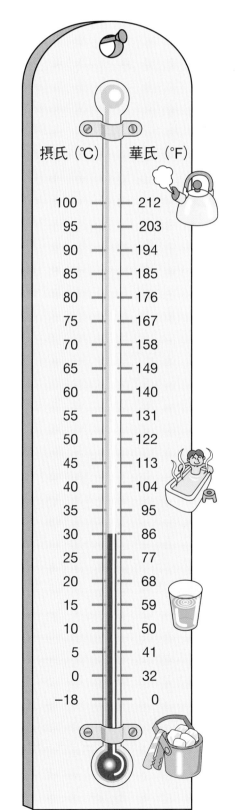

㉙ ■ WEATHER

	the sun It's sunny.		a cloud It's cloudy.
	rain It's rainy.		snow It's snowy.
	wind It's windy.		storm It's stormy.
	fog It's foggy.		thunder and lightning

㉚ How's the weather?

— It's [sunny / cloudy / rainy / snowy /
  windy / stormy / foggy / clear].

— There's thunder and lightning.

— It's [cold / cool / warm / hot / humid / dry].

❽ ENGLISH NUMBERS 数

㉜ ■ Cardinal Numbers & Ordinal Numbers 基数・序数

数	基　数	序　数
0	zero	
1	one	1st first
2	two	2nd second
3	three	3rd third
4	four	4th fourth
5	five	5th fifth
6	six	6th sixth
7	seven	7th seventh
8	eight	8th eighth
9	nine	9th ninth
10	ten	10th tenth
11	eleven	11th eleventh
12	twelve	12th twelfth
13	thirteen	13th thirteenth
14	fourteen	14th fourteenth
15	fifteen	15th fifteenth
16	sixteen	16th sixteenth
17	seventeen	17th seventeenth
18	eighteen	18th eighteenth
19	nineteen	19th nineteenth
20	twenty	20th twentieth
21	twenty-one	21st twenty-first
22	twenty-two	22nd twenty-second
23	twenty-three	23rd twenty-third
24	twenty-four	24th twenty-fourth
25	twenty-five	25th twenty-fifth
26	twenty-six	26th twenty-sixth
27	twenty-seven	27th twenty-seventh
28	twenty-eight	28th twenty-eighth
29	twenty-nine	29th twenty-ninth
30	thirty	30th thirtieth
40	forty	40th fortieth
50	fifty	50th fiftieth
60	sixty	60th sixtieth
70	seventy	70th seventieth
80	eighty	80th eightieth
90	ninety	90th ninetieth

数	基　数	序　数
100	one hundred	100th one hundredth
1,000	one thousand	1,000th one thousandth
10,000	ten thousand	10,000th ten thousandth
100,000	one hundred thousand	100,000th one hundred thousandth
1,000,000	one million	1,000,000th one millionth

㉝

数	読み方	意　味
200	two hundred	2×100
300	three hundred	3×100
1,000	one thousand	1×1000
1,100	one thousand one hundred eleven hundred	$1 \times 1,000 + 1 \times 100$ 11×100
1,200	one thousand two hundred twelve hundred	$1 \times 1,000 + 2 \times 100$ 12×100
2,000	two thousand	$2 \times 1,000$
2,100	two thousand one hundred twenty-one hundred	$2 \times 1,000 + 1 \times 100$ $(20 + 1) \times 100$

❾ PUNCTUATION MARKS　.　,　'　? & CAPITAL LETTERS　句読点・大文字

■ Punctuation Exercise.　Rewrite correctly.　(Hint: number of corrections needed)

〈Example〉 how do you do　(2)

　　　　　→ How do you do?

1. good morning ms suzuki　　hello everyone　(9)

_____

_____

2. how are you　　im fine thank you　　and you　(8)

_____

_____

3. tokyo is a big city　　is osaka a big city too　(6)

_____

_____

4. yes it is　　its a very big city　(6)

_____

_____

5. this is my new eraser　　do you have a new eraser too　　no i dont　(10)

_____

_____

ここでは，単語の意味は気にせず，モデルの発音をまねて英語の強弱，リズムの練習をしましょう.

❶ CONSONANTS（子音）1

㉞

[p] peach	[b] baby	[t] table	[d] dinner
please	bird	teach	dark
computer	bridge	notebook	drink
stop	umbrella	rocket	idea
sleep	club	heart	road

㉟

[k] kite	[g] girl	[m] make	[n] name
color	goal	moon	noisy
cup	green	home	dinosaur
clock	glass	smile	uniform
music	leg	alarm	train

㊱

◆Please pick up the peach.
◆The butterfly likes the baby bird.

◆That girl has a green glass.
◆The moon makes me smile.

◆(赤のダイヤモンド)の付いた英文には，うしろから単語を積みあげる方式の音声が吹きこまれています.

㊲

[l] leg	black	[r] rabbit	bread	[l/r] light / right
gorilla	class	eraser	dream	list / wrist
milk	flower	car	free	
sale	please	chair	green	
school	sleepy	teacher	train	

㊳

◆Left, right, left, right, left, right, left. Up, down, in, out, all around.
◆Lily's little purple turtle likes apples.

㊴

[f] fine	[v] very	[θ] thank	[ð] this
friend	vacation	Thursday	father
elephant	television	three	mother
beef	love	math	together
laugh	of	mouth	weather

㊵

◆Here are four fine fresh fish for you.
◆My friend laughs very loudly.

◆The bird's feather is smooth and thin.
◆They both took a bath at three.

CONSONANTS（子音）2

hard c	soft c (ce, ci, cy)	hard g	soft g (ge, gi, gy)	41
[k] car	[s] dance	[g] game	[dʒ] gentle	
cold	city	gold	giant	
cup	pencil	guitar	magic	
club	science	glove	engineer	
clock	cyber	leg	gym	

[w] wall	[kw] quiz	[j] yes	[h] happy	42
welcome	quiet	yo-yo	heart	
away	question	year	hint	
always	quit	yellow	house	
fireworks	square	yen	hunt	

[ŋ] ring	thing	[ŋg] angry		43
long	something	hungry		
young	everything	finger		
during	anything	kangaroo		
spring	nothing	mango		

[ʒ] television	[(h)w] what	[h] how		44
usually	when	who		
measure	where	whose		
Asia	which	whom		
garage	why	whole		

[h/f] horse / force
　　　hair / fair

[e/j]　　　s / yes　　44 45
[iər/jiər] ear / year

46
◆ The gentle giant plays in the gym with the gorilla. But the gorilla wants the guitar.

◆ That young kangaroo is very hungry. He eats everything.

Let's Say It

CONSONANTS (子音) 3

(47)
♦ There's a very hungry elephant at the zoo.
  No food?　Now he's very angry.
♦ Quick.　Answer the question.　Quiet.　Finish the quiz.
♦ Do children in Asia watch television after school?

(48)　[s]　street　　cent　　　　[z]　zero　　　newspaper
　　　　　sea　　　celery　　　　　　　zipper　　busy
　　　　　singer　　center　　　　　　　zoo　　　boys
　　　　　bus　　　pencil　　　　　　　size　　　clothes
　　　　　miss　　　face　　　　　　　quiz　　　shoes

(49)　[ʃ]　shop　　　　　　　　[tʃ]　child
　　　　　shoulder　　　　　　　　children
　　　　　fish　　　　　　　　　　sandwich
　　　　　push　　　　　　　　　　kitchen
　　　　　wash　　　　　　　　　　watch

(50)　[-s / -z]　ice　　/ eyes　　　[ʃ / s]　shoe　/ Sue
　　　　　　　　rice　　/ rise　　　　　　　　shoot / suit
　　　　　　　　race　　/ raise　　　　　　　sheet / seat
　　　　　　　　price / prize　　　　　　　shine / sign

(51)
♦ I see an icy street.　Be careful!
  — Oops! ... Ow ...
♦ What size shoes do you have?
  — Size twenty-six.
♦ Don't wash your watch in the washing machine.
♦ I see some children eating chicken in the kitchen.
♦ She sells seashells by the seashore.　She also sells delicious fish dishes.

❷ VOWELS（母音）1

52 [iː] eat   [i] ink   [iː / i] feet / fit
       speak   drink   seat / sit
       niece   big   team / Tim
       feet   sit   sheep / ship
       happy   winter   heat / hit

53
> ◆ Sit in the seat, please.
> ◆ Eat it in the evening.

> ◆ I see a little letter.
>   — Pick it up and put it in the PO Box.

54 [ei] April   [e] egg   [ei / e] late / let
       baby   bed   tail   / tell
       cake   bread   wait / wet
       day   seven   sale / sell
       eight   lesson   gate / get

55
> ◆ Mail the letter later.
> ◆ Meet me at the gate. And don't be late.
>   — At seven?
>   No, eight.

56 [æ] animal   [ʌ] uncle   [ɑ] office
       answer   cup   hot
       bag   bus   job
       hand   come   not
       rabbit   lunch   stop

57
> ◆ The rat ran faster than the fat cat.
> ◆ The farmer has a large new car.
> ◆ My mom stopped at a watch shop.

> ◆ Where's the egg?
>   — It's under the bed.

58 [æ / ɑ] cap / cop   [æ / ʌ] bat   / but   [ʌ / ɑ] cup / cop
            black / block   ankle / uncle   luck / lock
       [æ / ʌ / ɑ] cap / cup / cop
                  hat   / hut / hot

Let's Say It

VOWELS (母音) 2

⑤⑨ [ei / æ] ate / at   [e / æ] guess / gas

fate / fat   lend / land

hate / hat   said / sad

made / mad   met / mat

⑥⓪
- He ate an apple at night.
- Kate hates her hats.

- Please lend me a hand.
- He said she was sad.

⑥① [uː] soup   [u] book   [uː / u] food / full

blue   cook   pool / pull

shoe   foot   cooled / could

you   full

new   push

⑥②
- Do you want any food?
  - No, I'm full.
- A good cook reads the cookbook.

- Do you want to go to the zoo?
  - Yes, I do.
  - Me, too.
  - Me, three!

⑥③ [ou] old   [ɔː] ball   [ou / ɔː] cold / call

open   dog   bowl / ball

home   August   hole / hall

snow   walk

goal   draw

⑥④
- Walk slowly. Don't run.
- Let's play ball in the fall.

- Don't push me. Don't touch me. Hands off!
- Let's take a long walk and talk about it.

⑥⑤
- Open the door.   You do it.
  - Oh! Snow!   - Ooo! My shoes are new.

  Walk the dog.   Today?
  - Aw! Bring a ball.   - Eh? Yes, now I say.

VOWELS (母音) 3

⑥⑥ [ai] ice   [au] cow   [ɔi] oil

        high   about   join

        kind   hour   noisy

        time   count   boy

        buy   mouth   point

⑥⑦
- ◆ My aunt Aiko is very kind. She buys me ice cream every time.
- ◆ How about that cow?
  — The brown cow? Yes, I see it now.
- ◆ The noisy boy put oil in the toilet! Oh! Ah! Ew!

⑥⑧ [iər] ear   [eər] air   [ur] poor   [ɔr] or   [ɑr] art

     hear   bear   tour   door   heart

     deer   where   [jur] sure   four   large

     year   pair   pure   sport   farmer

     engineer   share   store   guitar

⑥⑨
- ◆ Roar! That's a rare bear.
- ◆ Don't stand there at the rear door.

- ◆ The art students draw hearts and stars.
- ◆ Can I go on a tour?
  — Sure.

⑦⓪ [ər] teacher   birthday   doctor   Thursday

     mother   circle   world   hurt

     river   girl   color   turn

     earth   first   elevator   future

     another   sir   neighbor   purple

⑦① [ɑr / ər] hard / heard
     [æ / ər] fast / first

- ◆ I heard that the test is hard.
- ◆ First, say this fast.

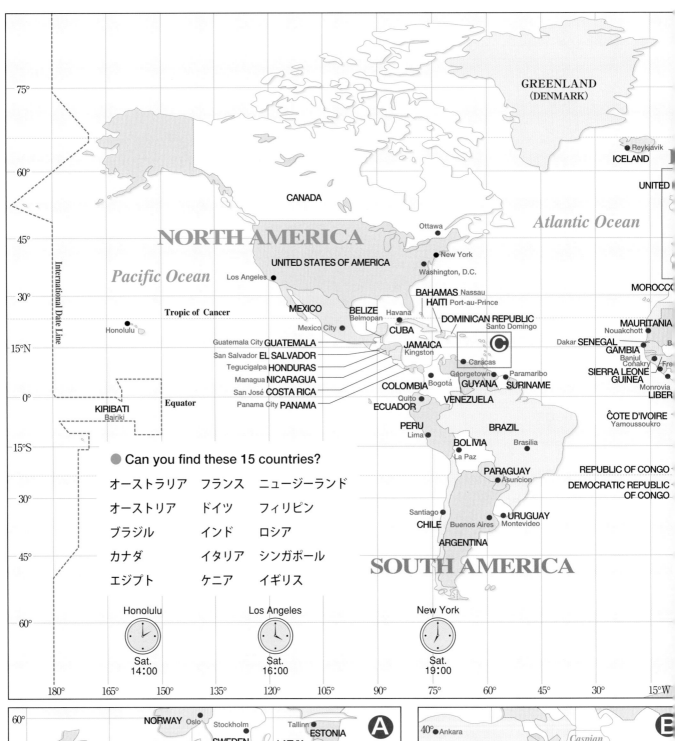

75°
60°
45°
30°
15°N
0°
15°S
30°
45°
60°

International Date Line

GREENLAND
(DENMARK)

Reykjavik
ICELAND

UNITED

Atlantic Ocean

CANADA

NORTH AMERICA

Pacific Ocean

Ottawa
New York
Washington, D.C.

UNITED STATES OF AMERICA

Los Angeles

MOROCCO

Tropic of Cancer

MEXICO

BAHAMAS   Nassau
HAITI   Port-au-Prince

BELIZE   Havana
Belmopan

DOMINICAN REPUBLIC
Santo Domingo

MAURITANIA
Nouakchott

Mexico City

CUBA

Dakar SENEGAL

Guatemala City GUATEMALA

JAMAICA

GAMBIA
Banjul

San Salvador EL SALVADOR

Kingston

Caracas

Conakry   Fre

Tegucigalpa HONDURAS

Georgetown   Paramaribo

SIERRA LEONE

Managua NICARAGUA

COLOMBIA   Bogotá

GUYANA   SURINAME

GUINEA

Monrovia

San José COSTA RICA

Quito

VENEZUELA

LIBER

Panama City PANAMA

ECUADOR

Equator

KIRIBATI
Bairiki

Honolulu

15°N

0°

PERU
Lima

BRAZIL

BOLIVIA
La Paz

Brasilia

CÔTE D'IVOIRE
Yamoussoukro

REPUBLIC OF CONGO

PARAGUAY
Asunción

DEMOCRATIC REPUBLIC
OF CONGO

● Can you find these 15 countries?

オーストラリア	フランス	ニュージーランド
オーストリア	ドイツ	フィリピン
ブラジル	インド	ロシア
カナダ	イタリア	シンガポール
エジプト	ケニア	イギリス

Santiago
CHILE

Buenos Aires

URUGUAY
Montevideo

ARGENTINA

SOUTH AMERICA

Honolulu

Sat.
14:00

Los Angeles

Sat.
16:00

New York

Sat.
19:00

180°   165°   150°   135°   120°   105°   90°   75°   60°   45°   30°   15°W

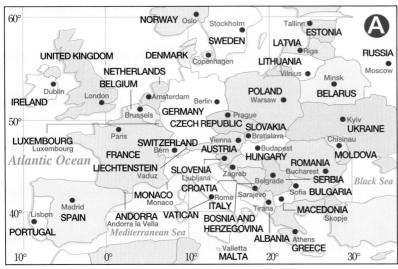

60°
NORWAY   Oslo   Stockholm
Tallinn
ESTONIA

SWEDEN   LATVIA
Riga
RUSSIA

UNITED KINGDOM   DENMARK
LITHUANIA
Moscow

NETHERLANDS   Copenhagen
Vilnius
Minsk

BELGIUM
POLAND
BELARUS

Dublin   London   Amsterdam   Berlin   Warsaw

IRELAND   Brussels   GERMANY   Prague   Kyiv

CZECH REPUBLIC   SLOVAKIA   UKRAINE

LUXEMBOURG   Paris   SWITZERLAND   Vienna   Bratislava   Chisinau

Luxembourg   FRANCE   Bern   AUSTRIA   HUNGARY   MOLDOVA

Atlantic Ocean   LIECHTENSTEIN   SLOVENIA   ROMANIA

Vaduz   Ljubljana   Zagreb   Belgrade   Bucharest   Black Sea

MONACO   CROATIA   Sarajevo   SERBIA

Madrid   Monaco   Rome   Sofia   BULGARIA

Lisbon   SPAIN   ANDORRA   ITALY   Tirana   MACEDONIA

PORTUGAL   Andorra la Vella   VATICAN   BOSNIA AND   Skopje

Mediterranean Sea   HERZEGOVINA   ALBANIA   Athens

Valletta   GREECE

10°   0°   10°   MALTA   20°   30°

40°

A

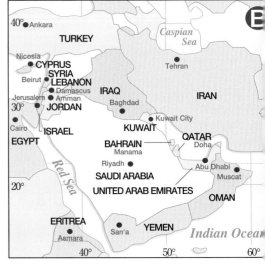

40°   Ankara

TURKEY

Caspian
Sea

Nicosia
CYPRUS
Tehran

Beirut   SYRIA
LEBANON

Jerusalem   Damascus   IRAQ   IRAN

30°   Amman   Baghdad

JORDAN

Cairo   ISRAEL   Kuwait City

EGYPT   BAHRAIN   KUWAIT   QATAR
Manama   Doha

Riyadh   Abu Dhabi
Muscat

20°   SAUDI ARABIA

UNITED ARAB EMIRATES   OMAN

Red Sea

ERITREA   YEMEN

San'a   Indian Ocean

Asmara

40°   50°   60°

B

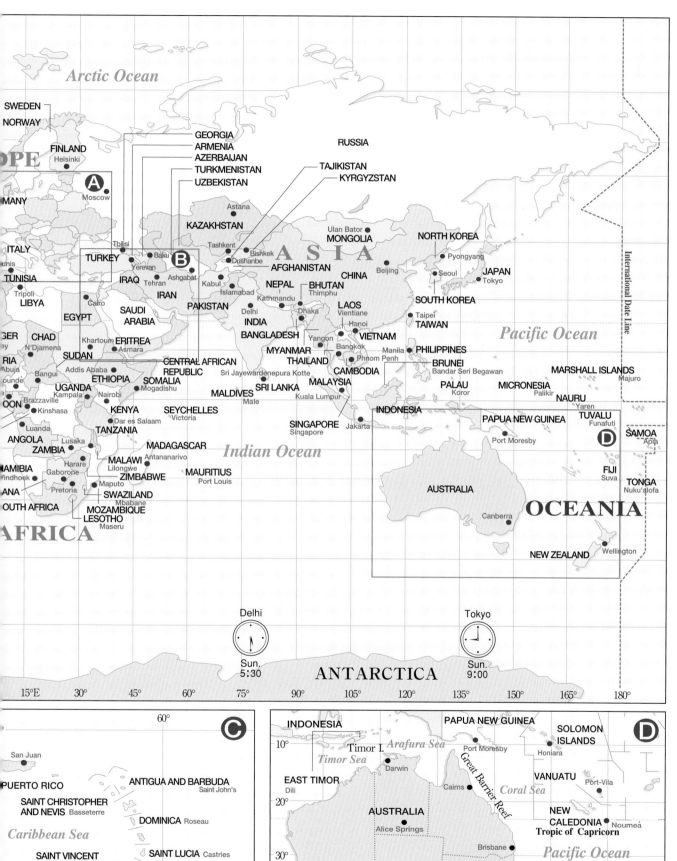

List of Words & Phrases

大文字ではじまる語句

カテゴリー別リスト

＊「授業や学校に関わる表現例」を含む

ABC 順リスト

● 黒字：『小学校外国語活動・外国語 研修ガイドブック』（文部科学省，2009)のカテゴリー分類1～17，授業や学校に関わる表現例に収録されている語句
● 青字：小学校英語検定教科書等から追加収録した語句およびカテゴリー分類18（主な連語）の語句

和英リスト

大文字ではじまる語句

DAYS

Sunday	日曜日
Monday	月曜日
Tuesday	火曜日
Wednesday	水曜日
Thursday	木曜日
Friday	金曜日
Saturday	土曜日

MONTHS

January	1月
February	2月
March	3月
April	4月
May	5月
June	6月
July	7月
August	8月
September	9月
October	10月
November	11月
December	12月

略語・短縮形

ALT	英語指導助手
CD player	CDプレーヤー
DVD player	DVDプレーヤー
P.E. / physical education	体育
PC / personal computer	パソコン
TV / television	テレビ
UFO / unidentified flying object	正体不明飛行物体
USB cable	USBケーブル
USB memory stick	USBメモリースティック
VCR / video cassette recorder	ビデオデッキ
I'd	= I would
Mr.	～さん(男性に対する敬称)
Ms.	～さん(女性に対する敬称)
Mt.	～山

A・B・C

American football	アメリカンフットボール
Assistant Language Teacher	英語指導助手
Boys' Festival	端午の節句
Colosseo (Colosseum)	コロッセウム

E・F・G

English	英語
French fries	フライドポテト
Girls' Festival	ひな祭り
the Great Wall	万里の長城

I・J

I	私は(が)
Japanese	日本語, 国語, 日本の
Japanese tea	日本茶

M・N・O・P・S・T・Y

the Milky Way	天の川
New Year's Day	元日
Olympic Games	オリンピック大会
Paralympic Games	パラリンピック大会
Parent Visitation Day	参観日
School Foundation Day	創立記念日
Snow Festival	雪祭り
Star Festival	七夕祭り
T-shirt	Tシャツ
YouTube	ユーチューブ
YouTuber	ユーチューバー

国・都市は，**カテゴリー分類 11.** (*p.48*)に掲載

カテゴリー別リスト

1. 動作

brush	みがく
buy	買う
call	呼ぶ
check	チェックする
clean	清掃する
climb	登る
cook	(料理を)作る，料理する
dance	踊る
do	する
draw	(線で)描く
drink	飲む
eat	食べる
enjoy	楽しむ
fly	飛ぶ
get	手に入れる
go	行く
have	持っている
help	助ける
hit	打つ
hop	ぴょんぴょんとぶ
join	入る
jump	とぶ
kick	蹴る
leave	出発する
like	好きである
live	住む
look	見る
love	大好きである
make	作る
meet	会う
plant	植える
play	(楽器を)ひく，(運動を)する
pop	ポンと鳴る
practice	練習する
pull	引く
put	置く
quit	～をやめる
read	読む
ride	乗る
run	走る
save	救う

see	見る
set	配置する
sing	歌う
sit	すわる
sleep	眠る
smile	ほほ笑む
speak	話す
spell	つづる
stand	立つ
stop	止まる
study	勉強する
swim	泳ぐ
take	取る
tap	軽くたたく
thank	感謝する
think	考える
touch	触れる
try	やってみる
turn	回る
visit	訪ねる
wake	目を覚ます
walk	歩く
want	欲しい
wash	洗う
watch	見る
ate	食べた(eat の過去形)
enjoyed	楽しんだ(enjoy の過去形)
pulled	引いた(pull の過去形)
saw	見た(see の過去形)
went	行った(go の過去形)

2. 状態・気持ち

active	活動している
beautiful	美しい
best	最もよい
big	大きい
bitter	苦い
busy	忙しい
closed	閉店した
cold	寒い，冷たい
cool	涼しい，かっこいい
delicious	おいしい

exciting	わくわくするような	traditional	伝統的な
famous	有名な	wonderful	すばらしい
fantastic	すばらしい	young	若い
fast	速く	angry	腹を立てて
favorite	お気に入りの	brave	勇ましい
fresh	新鮮な	cheerful	元気のいい
fun	楽しみ	cute	かわいい
funny	面白い	fine	元気な
furry	ふわふわの	friendly	人に親切な
hard	固い	gentle	優しい
hard	一生懸命に	good	よい
heavy	重い	great	すばらしい
high	高い	happy	幸せな
hot	暑い，辛い	hungry	お腹がすいた
interesting	面白い	kind	親切な
junior	年下の	sad	悲しい
light	軽い	scary	怖い
little	小さい	sleepy	眠い
long	長い	sorry	すまなく思って
lovely	すてきな	tired	疲れた
lucky	幸運な	care	注意，用心
many	たくさんの	kindness	親切
much	とてもたくさん	year(s) old	～歳
new	新しい		
nice	よい		
old	古い		

3. 飲食物

open	開いている	bacon	ベーコン
popular	人気のある	beef	牛肉
quiet	静かな	crab	カニ
right	正しい	egg	卵
round	丸い	fish	魚
salty	塩からい	food	食べ物
shiny	輝く	fruit	果物
short	短い	lobster	イセエビ
slow	おそい	meat	肉
small	小さい	noodle	めん類
soft	やわらかい	octopus	タコ
sour	すっぱい	pork	ブタ肉
special	特別な	tuna	マグロ
spicy	香辛料の効いた	curry	カレー
strong	強い	curry and rice	カレーライス
sweet	甘い	French fries	フライドポテト
tall	高い	fried chicken	フライドチキン
thirsty	のどが乾いた	grilled fish	焼き魚
tough	簡単にへこたれない	hamburger	ハンバーガー
		hot dog	ホットドッグ

macaroni	マカロニ	spinach	ホウレンソウ
nan	ナン(インド料理)	sweet potato	サツマイモ
omelet	オムレツ	turnip	カブ
pie	パイ	bread	パン
pizza	ピザ	cake	ケーキ
rice ball	おにぎり	cheese	チーズ
salad	サラダ	chocolate	チョコレート
soup	スープ	coffee	コーヒー
spaghetti	スパゲッティ	dessert	デザート
steak	ステーキ	donut	ドーナツ
(table) roll	ロールパン(テーブルロール)	ice cream	アイスクリーム
toast	トースト	jam	ジャム
apple	リンゴ	juice	ジュース
banana	バナナ	pancake	ホットケーキ
cherry	サクランボ	parfait	パフェ
grape	ブドウ	peanut	ピーナッツ
grapefruit	グレープフルーツ	popcorn	ポップコーン
kiwi fruit	キューウィフルーツ	pudding	プリン
lemon	レモン	rice	ごはん，米
mango	マンゴー	sandwich	サンドイッチ
melon	メロン	shaved ice	かき氷
orange	オレンジ	snack	軽食
peach	モモ	drink	飲み物
pear	ナシ	milk	牛乳
pineapple	パイナップル	mineral water	ミネラルウォーター
strawberry	イチゴ	soda	ソーダ
tomato	トマト	tea	茶, 紅茶
watermelon	スイカ	water	水
asparagus	アスパラガス	oil	油
bean	豆	salt	塩
boiled vegetable	ゆで野菜	soy sauce	しょうゆ
cabbage	キャベツ	sugar	砂糖
carrot	ニンジン	vinegar	酢
celery	セロリ	fork	フォーク
chili	トウガラシ	knife	ナイフ
corn	トウモロコシ		

4. 数

zero	ゼロ
one	1
first, 1st	1番目(の)
two	2
second, 2nd	2番目(の)
three	3
third, 3rd	3番目(の)

cucumber	キュウリ	
eggplant	ナス	
green pepper	ピーマン	
lettuce	レタス	
mushroom	マッシュルーム	
nut	木の実	
onion	タマネギ	
potato	ジャガイモ	
radish	ハツカダイコン	

four	4
fourth, 4th	4番目(の)
five	5
fifth, 5th	5番目(の)
six	6
sixth, 6th	6番目(の)
seven	7
seventh, 7th	7番目(の)
eight	8
eighth, 8th	8番目(の)
nine	9
ninth, 9th	9番目(の)
ten	10
tenth, 10th	10番目(の)
eleven	11
eleventh, 11th	11番目(の)
twelve	12
twelfth, 12th	12番目(の)
thirteen	13
thirteenth, 13th	13番目(の)
fourteen	14
fourteenth, 14th	14番目(の)
fifteen	15
fifteenth, 15th	15番目(の)
sixteen	16
sixteenth, 16th	16番目(の)
seventeen	17
seventeenth, 17th	17番目(の)
eighteen	18
eighteenth, 18th	18番目(の)
nineteen	19
nineteenth, 19th	19番目(の)
twenty	20
twentieth, 20th	20番目(の)
thirty	30
thirtieth, 30th	30番目(の)
forty	40
fifty	50
sixty	60
seventy	70
eighty	80
ninety	90
hundred	100
thousand	1,000
yen	円(日本の通貨単位)

dollar	ドル(米国・カナダ・オーストラリア等の通貨単位)
cent	セント(米国・カナダ・オーストラリア等の通貨補助単位)

5. 学校生活

(1) 科目等

alphabet	アルファベット
art	芸術
arts and crafts	図画工作
calligraphy	書写
cooking	調理
fine arts	美術
foreign language activities	外国語活動
home economics	家庭科
industrial arts and home economics	技術・家庭科
math / mathematics	数学
moral education	道徳
music	音楽
period for integrated study	総合的な学習の時間
physical education / P.E.	体育
science	理科
social studies	社会科
special activities	特別活動
subject	教科

(2) 部屋・場所等

boys' room	男子トイレ
broadcasting room	放送室
bulletin board	掲示板
class	授業, 学級
classroom	教室
computer room	コンピュータ室
cooking room	調理室
courtyard	中庭
entrance	玄関
first floor	1階
girls' room	女子トイレ
gym	体育館
hallway	廊下
hand washing area	手洗い場
hand washing sink	手洗い場
junior high school	中学校
library	図書館
meeting room	会議室
music room	音楽室
notice board	掲示板
nurse's office	保健室

office	事務所	picture book	絵本
parking lot	駐車場	picture card	絵カード
playground	運動場	projector	プロジェクター
principal's office	校長室	ruler	定規
restroom	トイレ	scissors	ハサミ
rooftop	屋上	stapler	ホッチキス
room	部屋	tablet	タブレットパソコン
school	学校	textbook	教科書, テキスト
science room	理科室	thumbtack	画びょう
second floor	2階	video cassette recorder	ビデオデッキ
stairs	階段	worksheet	ワークシート
storage room	倉庫		
swimming pool	プール	**(5) 学校行事等**	
teachers' [office / room]	職員室	brass band	ブラスバンド
washroom	トイレ	chorus	合唱部
		chorus contest	合唱コンテスト
(3) 職員等		class activities	学級活動
board of education	教育委員会	class monitor duties	係活動
nursery school teacher	幼稚園の先生	cleaning	掃除
principal	校長	closing ceremony	終業式
school nurse	養護教諭	club	クラブ
school secretary	学校事務員	club activities	クラブ活動
student	生徒	cooking club	料理部
supervisor of school education	指導主事	cultural festival	文化祭
teacher	教師	demonstration lesson	研究授業
vice principal	教頭／副校長	drama festival	学芸会
		entrance ceremony	入学式
(4) 教材・教具等		event	行事
blackboard	黒板	field trip	遠足
crayon	クレヨン	first term	1学期
dice	サイコロ	general student meeting	生徒総会
digital picture book	デジタル絵本	graduation ceremony	卒業式
digital textbook	デジタル教科書	home visit	家庭訪問
eraser	消しゴム, 黒板消し	homeroom	ホームルーム（の時間/教室）
electronic whiteboard	電子ホワイトボード	lesson	授業
finger puppet	指人形	lesson plan	指導案
glue stick	スティックのり	morning assembly	（生徒の）朝礼
hand puppet	指人形	morning meeting for teachers	（教師の）朝会
ink	インク	music festival	音楽祭
letter	手紙	observation lesson	研究授業
marker	マーカー	open day	参観日
notebook	ノート	open house	授業参観
overhead camera	OHC，書画カメラ	open school	授業参観
pen	ペン	opening ceremony	始業式
pencil	エンピツ	parent-teacher meeting	個人懇談
pencil case	筆箱	recess	休み時間
pencil sharpener	エンピツ削り		

school lunch	給食	post	郵便
school trip	修学旅行	post office	郵便局
second term	2学期	restaurant	レストラン
speech contest	スピーチコンテスト	road	道路
sports day	運動会	sale	大売り出し
sports festival	運動会	shrine	神社
staff meeting	職員会議	sports shop	スポーツ用品店
student committee activities	委員会活動	stadium	スタジアム
student council	生徒会	station	駅
summer camp	サマーキャンプ	street	通り
swim(ming) meet	水泳大会	supermarket	スーパーマーケット
question	質問	temple	寺
answer	答	town	町
quiz	小テスト	zoo	動物園
term tests	期末テスト	airplane	飛行機
third term	3学期	boat	ボート，船
volunteer day	ボランティア活動の日	bus	バス
		car	自動車

6. 町・施設・職業

amusement park	遊園地	jet plane	ジェット機
aquarium	水族館	roller coaster	ジェットコースター
bank	銀行	ship	船
block	街区，ブロック	taxi	タクシー
bookstore	書店，本屋	train	列車
bridge	橋	van	小型トラック
castle	城	yacht	ヨット
convenience store	コンビニエンスストア	actor	俳優
corner	角，すみ	artist	芸術家
department store	デパート	astronaut	宇宙飛行士
exit	出口	baker	パン屋(人)
fire station	消防署	baseball player	野球選手
flower shop	花屋	bus driver	バスの運転手
garden	庭園	carpenter	大工
gas station	ガソリンスタンド	comedian	お笑い芸人
gate	門	cook	コック，料理人
hospital	病院	dentist	歯医者
hot spring	温泉	designer	デザイナー
house	家	doctor	医師
menu	メニュー	engineer	技術者
movie	映画	farmer	農業従事者
movie theater	映画館	firefighter	消防士
museum	博物館	flight attendant	客室乗務員
park	公園	florist	花屋(人)
pet shop	ペットショップ	game creator	ゲームクリエーター
police station	警察署	hairdresser	美容師
		hero	ヒーロー，あこがれの対象

illustrator	イラストレーター
job	仕事
king	王
musician	音楽家
nurse	看護師
pastry chef	パティシエ
people	人々
performer	出演者
pilot	パイロット
player	選手，演奏する人
police officer	警察官
queen	女王
singer	歌手
soccer player	サッカー選手
teacher	教師
train conductor	列車の車掌
vet	獣医
zookeeper	動物園の飼育係

7. 日常生活

activity	活動
alarm (clock)	目覚まし時計
apron	エプロン
bath	ふろ
bed	ベッド
bicycle	自転車
bike	自転車
book	本
box	箱
calendar	カレンダー
chair	いす
cleaning	掃除
clock	掛け時計
computer	コンピュータ
cup	カップ
desk	机
dish	皿
garbage	ゴミ
home	家
homework	宿題
key	かぎ
ladder	はしご
life	生活
magnet	マグネット
mailbox	郵便ポスト

map	地図
mat	マット
mochi making festival	もちつき大会
net	あみ
newspaper	新聞
note	メモ
outlet	コンセント
pan	ひらなべ
personal computer	パソコン
picture	写真
pot	なべ
ring	指輪
routines	日課
table	テーブル
telephone / phone	電話
umbrella	かさ
vase	花瓶
wall	壁
bag	かばん
boots	ブーツ
cap	(ふちのない)ぼうし
denim	デニム
gloves	グローブ
hat	(ふちのある)ぼうし
jeans	ジーンズ
pants	ズボン
rain boots	雨靴
raincoat	レインコート
shirt	シャツ
shorts	ショートパンツ
sneakers	スニーカー
sweater	セーター
watch	腕時計
wheelchair	車いす
zipper	ファスナー
drum	ドラム
guitar	ギター
piano	ピアノ
recorder	リコーダー
violin	バイオリン
breakfast	朝食
lunch	昼食
dinner	夕食

8. スポーツ

archery	アーチェリー
athletics	運動競技
badminton	バドミントン
baseball	野球
basketball	バスケットボール
boccia	ボッチャ
boxing	ボクシング
canoe	カヌー
climbing	登山
cricket	クリケット
cycling	サイクリング
dancing	ダンス
dodgeball	ドッジボール
fencing	フェンシング
football	フットボール
golf	ゴルフ
golfer	ゴルファー
gymnastics	体操競技
handball	ハンドボール
hockey	ホッケー
judo	柔道
lacrosse	ラクロス
rugby	ラグビー
sailing	セーリング
skate	スケートをする
skater	スケート選手
skating	スケート
ski	スキーをする
skier	スキー選手
skiing	スキー
snowboarding	スノーボード
soccer	サッカー
softball	ソフトボール
sumo	すもう
surf	サーフィンをする
surfer	サーファー
surfing	サーフィン
swimmer	水泳選手
swimming	水泳
swimwear	水着
table tennis	卓球
tennis	テニス
track and field	陸上競技
volleyball	バレーボール

weight lifting	重量挙げ
wheelchair basketball	車いすバスケットボール
wheelchair tennis	車いすテニス
wrestling	レスリング
sport	スポーツ
team	チーム
bat	バット
uniform	ユニフォーム
racket	ラケット

9. 色・形

black	黒色
blue	青色
brown	茶色
color	色
green	緑色
light blue	薄い青色
orange	オレンジ色
pink	ピンク色
purple	紫色
red	赤色
white	白色
yellow	黄色
circle	円
cross	十字形
diamond	ダイアモンド形
heart	ハート型，心，心臓
rectangle	長方形
square	四角形
star	星形
triangle	三角形

10. 季節・時間　　月・曜日は *p.39*

season	季節
spring	春
summer	夏
autumn	秋
fall	秋
winter	冬
time	時刻
day	日
month	月
year	年
morning	朝，午前中
afternoon	午後

a.m.	午前〜時
p.m.	午後〜時
now	今
today	今日(は)
past	過去

11. 国・都市

COUNTRY / COUNTRIES　国

Australia	オーストラリア
Brazil	ブラジル
Canada	カナダ
China	中国
Egypt	エジプト
France	フランス
Germany	ドイツ
Greece	ギリシャ
India	インド
Italy	イタリア
Japan	日本
Kenya	ケニア
Korea	韓国，朝鮮
Mexico	メキシコ
Mongolia	モンゴル
Morocco	モロッコ
New Zealand	ニュージーランド
Peru	ペルー
Russia	ロシア
Spain	スペイン
Switzerland	スイス
Thailand	タイ
the UK	イギリス
the USA	アメリカ合衆国

CITY / CITIES　都市

Honolulu	ホノルル
London	ロンドン
Nairobi	ナイロビ
New Delhi	ニューデリー
Rio de Janeiro	リオデジャネイロ
Sydney	シドニー
Vancouver	バンクーバー

12. 動植物

animal	動物
bear	クマ
bird	鳥

boar	イノシシ
cat	ネコ
chicken	ニワトリ
cow	雌牛，(特に)乳牛
dog	イヌ
dolphin	イルカ
elephant	ゾウ
flamingo	フラミンゴ
fox	キツネ
goat	ヤギ
gorilla	ゴリラ
hen	めんどり
horse	ウマ
koala	コアラ
lion	ライオン
monkey	サル
mouse	ネズミ
owl	フクロウ
ox	雄牛
panda	パンダ
penguin	ペンギン
pig	ブタ
rabbit	ウサギ
raccoon dog	タヌキ
rat	ネズミ
rooster	おんどり
sheep	ヒツジ
snake	ヘビ
tiger	トラ
wild boar	イノシシ
zebra	シマウマ
ant	アリ
bee	ハチ
beetle	カブトムシ
bug	昆虫
butterfly	チョウ
dragonfly	トンボ
frog	カエル
grasshopper	キリギリス，バッタ
insect	昆虫
moth	蛾(ガ)
spider	蜘蛛(クモ)
dinosaur	恐竜
dragon	ドラゴン，竜
flower	花

nest	巣
tree	木
log	丸太
wood	木材

13. 自然・天気

beach	浜辺
desert	砂漠
island	島
lake	湖
mountain	山
river	川
sea	海
open sea(s)	大海，外洋
star	星
sun	太陽
top	頂上
cloudy	くもりの
rainy	雨の
snowy	雪の
sunny	晴れの
twinkle	きらきら光る
windy	風の強い
nature	自然
rainbow	虹
weather	天気

14. 祝祭日・趣味・遊び

barbeque	バーベキュー
camping	キャンプ
festival	祭り
fireworks	花火
fishing	魚釣り
hiking	ハイキング
jogging	ジョギング
parade	パレード
playing	遊ぶこと，プレーすること
reading	読書
shopping	買い物
song	歌
trip	旅行
vacation	休暇
ball	ボール
bingo	ビンゴ
card	カード

doll	人形
game	ゲーム
jump rope	なわとびの縄
kite	凧
marble	ビー玉，大理石
tag	鬼ごっこ
unicycle	一輪車
yo-yo	ヨーヨー

15. 人と身体

I	私は(が)
my	私の
me	私に(を)
you	あなた(は，が，を)
your	あなたの
you're	= you are
yourself	あなた自身
we	私たちは(が)
our	私たちの
us	私たちに
he	彼は(が)
she	彼女は(が)
family	家族
boy	少年
girl	少女
father	父
mother	母
brother	兄・弟
sister	姉・妹
friend	友だち
grandfather	祖父
grandmother	祖母
grandparents	祖父母
aunt	おば
uncle	おじ
cousin	いとこ
baby	赤ん坊
ear	耳
eye	目
face	顔
hair	髪の毛
hand	手
head	頭
knee	ひざ
leg	脚

lip	くちびる		can't	= cannot
mouth	口		do	助動詞
nose	鼻		don't	= do not
shoulder	肩		would	〜でしょう
teeth	歯（tooth の複数形）		about	〜について
toe	足の指		around	〜のあちこちに
voice	声		at	〜に
wig	かつら		by	〜のそばに

16. その他（抽象語）

birthday	誕生日		for	〜のために
culture	文化		from	〜から
dream	夢		in	〜の中に
future	未来		inside	〜の中に
goal	ゴール		of	〜の
hint	ヒント		on	〜（の上）に
idea	考え		outside	外は
luck	運		to	〜へ
memory	思い出		under	〜の下に
name	名前		with	〜と一緒に
news	ニュース		again	もう一度
nickname	ニックネーム		all	すべて
party	パーティー		always	いつも
peace	平和		away	離れて
place	場所		down	座って
start	スタート		here	ここに
step	一歩		never	決して〜ない
stroke	ストローク，ひとかき		not	〜でない
treasure	宝物		off	離れて
world	世界		out	外へ
left	左，左に(の)		really	本当に
right	右，右に(の)		so	さて
straight	まっすぐに		up	上へ

17. その他（ことば）

			sometimes	ときどき
			usually	たいてい
			very	たいへん
			well	じょうずに
a	1つの		what	何を
an	1つの		what's	= what is
the	その		when	いつ
be	〜である（am, is, are の原形）		where	どこへ
am	（私は）〜です		who	だれ
are	〜です		why	なぜ
is	〜です		how	どのくらい
was	= am, is の過去形		how's	= how is
were	= are の過去形		and	そして，〜と
can	〜できる		because	〜なので

but	しかし
it	それは(が)
it's	= it is
this	これは(が)
that	それは(が)
that's	= that is
they	彼らは(が)，それらは(が)
goodbye	さようなら
hello	こんにちは
hi	やあ
yes	はい
no	いいえ
let's	～しようか
please	どうか，どうぞ
welcome	ようこそ

18. 主な連語

be famous for	～で有名である
be from	～出身
be good at	～がじょうず
do my homework	宿題をする
enjoy ～ing	～することを楽しむ
feed the dog	イヌにエサをやる
get the newspaper	新聞を取ってくる

get up	起きる
go home	帰宅する
go to bed	寝る
look at	～を見る
set the table	食事の準備をする
take a bath	ふろに入る
take out the garbage	ゴミを出す
take pictures	写真を撮る
walk my dog	イヌの散歩をする
wash the dishes	皿洗いをする
water the flowers	花に水をやる
Happy New Year	新年おめでとう
Here you are.	はい，ここにあります．
How much is ～?	(値段をたずねて)いくらですか．
I'd like ～.	～をお願いします．
Long time no see.	お久しぶりです．
Nice to meet you.	はじめまして．
No, thank you.	いいえ，結構です．
Take care of yourself.	お大事に．
Take care.	気をつけて．
Thank you for ～.	～をありがとう．
What do you do?	職業は何ですか．
You're welcome.	どういたしまして．

ABC順リスト

（1）数字は『研修ガイドブック』のカテゴリー分類を示し，新たに「カテゴリー18」（主な連語30項目）*pp.51-52*を加えた.

（2）黒字は『研修ガイドブック』の収録語句，青字は小学校検定教科書等から追加した語句およびカテゴリー分類18の語句を示す.

（3）大文字ではじまる語句は，カテゴリー分類外とし，0（ゼロ）で示す.

（4）コンマは，語順をかえて見出しとして掲載されていることを示す.（数詞，No のあとのコンマを除く）
例：take a bath は，イタリクス体を用い *a bath, take* および *bath, take a* としても掲載する.

A

a	17
a bath, take	18
a.m.	10
about	17
active	2
activities, class	5
activities, club	5
activities, foreign language	5
activities, special	5
activities, student committee	5
activity	7
actor	6
afternoon	10
again	17
airplane	6
alarm	7
all	17
alphabet	5
ALT	0
always	17
am	17
American football	0
amusement park	6
an	17
and	17
angry	2
animal	12
ant	12
apple	3
April	0
apron	7
aquarium	6
archery	8
are	17

area, hand washing	5
around	17
art	5
artist	6
arts and crafts	5
arts and home economics, industrial	5
asparagus	3
assembly, morning	5
Assistant Language Teacher	0
astronaut	6
at	17
at, look	18
ate	1
athletics	8
attendant, flight	6
August	0
aunt	15
Australia	11
autumn	10
away	17

B

baby	15
bacon	3
badminton	8
bag	7
baker	6
ball	14
ball, rice	3
banana	3
band, brass	5
bank	6
barbeque	14
baseball	8

baseball player	6
basketball	8
basketball, wheelchair	8
bat	8
bath	7
bath, take a	18
be	17
be famous for	18
be from	18
be good at	18
beach	13
bean	4
bear	12
beautiful	2
because	17
bed	7
bed, go to	18
bee	12
beef	3
beetle	12
best	2
bicycle	7
big	2
bike	7
bingo	14
bird	12
birthday	16
bitter	2
black	9
blackboard	5
block	6
blue	9
blue, light	9
boar	12
boar, wild	12

hundred	4	**K**		Long time no see.	18
hungry	2	Kenya	11	look	1
		key	7	look at	18
I		kick	1	*lot, parking*	5
I	0, 15	kind	2	love	1
I'd	0	kindness	2	lovely	2
I'd like ~.	18	king	6	luck	16
ice cream	3	kite	14	lucky	2
ice, shaved	3	kiwi fruit	3	lunch	7
idea	16	knee	15	*lunch, school*	5
illustrator	6	knife	3		
in	17	koala	12	**M**	
India	11	Korea	11	macaroni	3
industrial arts and				magnet	7
home economics	5	**L**		mailbox	7
ink	5	lacrosse	8	make	1
insect	12	ladder	7	mango	3
inside	17	lake	13	many	2
integrated study, period for	5	*language activities, foreign*	5	map	7
interesting	2	leave	1	marble	14
is	17	left	16	March	0
island	13	leg	15	marker	5
it	17	lemon	3	mat	7
it's	17	lesson	5	math	5
Italy	11	lesson plan	5	mathematics	5
		lesson, demonstration	5	May	0
J		*lesson, observation*	5	me	15
jam	3	let's	17	meat	3
January	0	letter	5	meet	1
Japan	11	lettuce	3	*meet, swim(ming)*	5
Japanese	0	library	5	*meeting for teachers, morning*	5
Japanese tea	0	life	7	meeting room	5
jeans	7	*lifting, weight*	8	*meeting, general student*	5
jet plane	6	light	2	*meeting, parent-teacher*	5
job	6	light blue	9	*meeting, staff*	5
jogging	14	like	1	melon	3
join	1	*like ~., I'd*	18	memory	16
judo	8	lion	12	*memory stick, USB*	0
juice	3	lip	15	menu	6
July	0	little	2	Mexico	11
jump	1	live	1	milk	3
jump rope	14	lobster	3	mineral water	3
June	0	log	12	*mochi* making festival	7
junior	2	London	11	Monday	0
junior high school	5	long	2	Mongolia	11

school teacher, nursery	5	sixteen	4	sports day	5
school trip	5	sixteenth, 16th	4	sports festival	5
school, junior high	5	sixth, 6th	4	sports shop	6
school, open	5	sixty	4	spring	10
science	5	skate	8	*spring, hot*	6
science room	5	skater	8	square	9
scissors	5	skating	8	stadium	6
sea	13	ski	8	staff meeting	5
sea, open	13	skier	8	stairs	5
season	10	skiing	8	stand	1
second floor	5	sleep	1	stapler	5
second term	5	sleepy	2	star	9, 13
second, 2nd	4	slow	2	Star Festival	0
secretary, school	5	small	2	start	16
see	1	smile	1	station	6
see., Long time no	18	snack	3	*station, fire*	6
September	0	snake	12	*station, gas*	6
set	1	sneakers	7	*station, police*	6
set the table	18	Snow Festival	0	steak	3
seven	4	snowboarding	8	step	16
seventeen	4	snowy	13	*stick, glue*	5
seventeenth, 17th	4	so	17	*stick, USB memory*	0
seventh, 7th	4	soccer	8	stop	1
seventy	4	soccer player	6	storage room	5
sharpener, pencil	5	social studies	5	*store, convenience*	6
shaved ice	3	soda	3	*store, department*	6
she	15	soft	2	straight	16
sheep	12	softball	8	strawberry	3
shiny	2	sometimes	17	street	6
ship	6	song	14	stroke	16
shirt	7	sorry	2	strong	2
shop, flower	6	soup	3	student	5
shop, pet	6	sour	2	student committee activities	5
shop, sports	6	soy sauce	3	student council	5
shopping	14	spaghetti	3	*student meeting, general*	5
short	2	Spain	11	*studies, social*	5
shorts	7	speak	1	study	1
shoulder	15	special	2	*study, period for integrated*	5
shrine	6	special activities	5	subject	5
sing	1	speech contest	5	sugar	3
singer	6	spell	1	sumo	8
sink, hand washing	5	spicy	2	summer	10
sister	15	spider	12	summer camp	5
sit	1	spinach	3	sun	13
six	4	sport	8	Sunday	0

和英リスト

Birdland English Course Unit I Revised Edition *pp.219-223* から転載

動　詞　＊は不規則動詞

あ行

会う	meet ＊
与える	give ＊
洗う	wash
歩く	walk
言う	say ＊
行く	go ＊
いないのを さみしく思う	miss
失う	lose ＊
うそをつく	lie
10 歌う	sing ＊
撃つ	shoot ＊
運転する	drive ＊
エサをあげる	feed ＊
選ぶ	choose ＊
得る	get ＊
置く	put ＊
送る	send ＊
起こす	wake ＊
教える	teach ＊
20 落ちる	fall ＊
覚える	remember
思う	think ＊

か行

買う	buy ＊
描く	draw ＊
書く	write ＊
勝つ	win ＊
かむ	bite ＊
感謝する	thank
聞く	hear ＊
30	listen
競技をする	play
切る	cut ＊
来る	come ＊
航海する	sail
答える	answer
ゴールする	finish

壊す	break ＊

さ行

させる	let ＊
知っている	know ＊
出発する	leave ＊
招待する	invite
心配する	worry
好き	like
住む	live
する	do ＊
10 座る	sit ＊
掃除する	clean

た行

大好きである	love
尋ねる	ask
訪ねる	visit
楽しむ	enjoy
食べる	eat ＊
	have ＊
試す	try
ついて行く	follow
20 使う	use
つかまえる	catch ＊
作る	make ＊
手伝う	help
閉じる	close
とどまる	stay
飛ぶ	fly ＊
とる	take ＊

な行

泣く	cry
鳴る	ring ＊
30 寝過ごす	oversleep ＊
眠る	sleep ＊
望む	wish
飲む	drink ＊
乗りそこなう	miss

乗る	ride ＊

は行

始める	begin ＊
	start
走る	run ＊
話す	speak ＊
	talk
	tell ＊
引っ張る	pull
必要とする	need
10 ひどく嫌う	hate
勉強する	study
欲しい	want

ま行

待つ	wait
学ぶ	learn
回す	pass
みがく	brush
見つける	find ＊
見る	look
	see ＊
20	watch
持って行く	bring ＊
持っている	have ＊

や行

焼く	bake
約束する	promise
読む	read ＊

ら行

理解する	understand ＊
料理する	cook
練習する	practice

わ行

忘れる	forget ＊
30 笑う	laugh

形容詞

あ行

明るい	bright
温かい	warm
新しい	new
暑い	hot
厚い	thick
甘い	sweet
雨降りの	rainy
忙しい	busy
一番好きな	favorite
10 いっぱいの	full
いつもの	usual
うすい	thin
美しい	beautiful
大きい	big
	large
遅れた	late
遅い	slow
お腹がすいている	hungry
重い	heavy
20 面白い	funny
	interesting

か行

風の強い	windy
かたい	hard
悲しい	sad
	unhappy
空の	empty
かわいい	cute
	pretty
かわいそうな	poor
30 簡単な	easy
汚い	dirty
奇妙な	strange
巨大な	huge
国の	national

曇った	cloudy
暗い	dark

さ行

最新の	latest
寒い	cold
幸せな	happy
静かな	quiet
親しく接してくる	friendly
湿気の多い	humid
自由な	free
10 重要な	important
主要な	main
準備のできた	ready
私立の	private
親切な	kind
涼しい	cool
すてきな	nice
すばらしい	great
	wonderful
清潔な	clean

た行

20 (背が)高い	tall
高い	high
ただ1人の	only
小さい	little
	small
注意深い	careful
疲れた	tired
月々の	monthly
次の	next
強い	strong
30 特別な	special

な行

長い	long

人気のある	popular
ねむい	sleepy
のどがかわいた	thirsty

は行

ばかな	stupid
恥ずかしがりの	shy
速い	fast
晴れた	fine
半分の	half
左の	left
10 費用のかかる	expensive
開いている	open
広い	wide
深い	deep
太った	fat
古い	old
他の	other

ま行

まじめな	serious
魔法の	magic
丸い	round
20 マンガ本	comic book
右の	right
短い	short
難しい	difficult

や行

やかましい	noisy
役に立つ	useful
安い	cheap
やわらかい	soft
有名な	famous
よい	good

名詞

あ行

愛称	nickname
アイスクリーム	ice cream
赤ちゃん	baby

明かり	light
秋	autumn
	fall
足	foot

脚	leg
アヒル	duck
アマツバメ	swift
アリ	ant

家	house	科学	science	協力	cooperation
池	pond	鏡	mirror	銀行	bank
医者	doctor	学生	student	近所の人	neighbor
イチゴ	strawberry	学年	grade	クジラ	whale
一輪車	unicycle	掛け時計	clock	薬	medicine
一歩	step	かご	basket	果物	fruit
いとこ	cousin	かさ	umbrella	くちびる	lip
イヌ	dog	歌手	singer	靴	shoe
イベント	event	かぜ	cold	クッキー	cookie
10 Eメール	email	10 型	type	10 国	country
イモムシ	caterpillar	カタツムリ	snail	組（1セット）	pair
色	color	学校	school	クモ（蜘蛛）	spider
ウサギ	rabbit	活動	activity	クラス	class
歌	song	カップ	cup	クラブ	club
腕	arm	角	corner	車	car
腕時計	watch	カード	card	警察	police
ウマ	horse	カバン	bag	ケーキ	cake
運転手	driver	花びん	vase	劇	play
運動場	playground	カフェテリア	cafeteria	結婚式	wedding
20 絵	picture	20 壁	wall	20 ゲーム	game
駅	station	カボチャ	pumpkin	県	prefecture
エンジニア	engineer	髪	hair	言語	language
エンジン	engine	紙	paper	健康	health
エンドウ豆	pea	カラス	crow	語	word
尾	tail	川	river	コアラ	koala
おい	nephew	カンガルー	kangaroo	コイ（鯉）	carp
雄牛	ox	感謝	thanks	公園	park
オウム	parrot	木	tree	子牛	calf
お金	money		wood	紅茶	tea
30 贈り物	gift	30 機械	machine	30 氷	ice
おじ	uncle	季節	season	故郷	hometown
オタマジャクシ	tadpole	ギター	guitar	黒板	blackboard
驚き	surprise	キツネ	fox	コーチ	coach
おば	aunt	切符	ticket	コップ	glass
おみやげ	souvenir	客	guest	コート	court
おもちゃ	toy	キャンプ	camp	子ども	child
オレンジ（果物）	orange	休暇	vacation	ことわざ	proverb
音楽	music	球根	bulb	コーヒー	coffee
		休日	holiday	ゴルフ	golf
か行		40 牛乳	milk	40 コンサート	concert
階	floor	教科書	textbook	昆虫	insect
40 買い物	shopping	教師	teacher	コンピュータ	computer
カエル	frog	教室	classroom		
顔	face	競走馬	racehorse	**さ行**	
画家	painter	兄弟	brother	サイクリング	cycling

菜食主義者	vegetarian
さお	pole
魚	fish
サクラ	cherry blossom
作家	writer
サッカー	soccer
雑誌	magazine
砂糖	sugar
サーフィン	surfing
10 皿	dish
サル	monkey
サンドイッチ	sandwich
塩	salt
歯科医	dentist
時間	hour
時間割	schedule
試験	test
仕事	job
	work
20 シチュー	stew
実験室	lab
質問	question
自転車	bike
シーフード	seafood
島	island
姉妹	sister
事務所	office
ジャガイモ	potato
写真	photo
30 シャツ	shirt
ジャーナリスト	journalist
州	state
集会	assembly
住所	address
ジュース	juice
週末	weekend
宿題	homework
受賞者	winner
順番	turn
40 商業	business
少女	girl
小説	fiction
冗談	joke
小テスト	quiz
少年	boy

ジョギング	jogging
女性	female
	woman
書店	bookstore
人口	population
信号音	tone
真実	truth
親戚	relative
新婦	bride
10 新聞	newspaper
新郎	groom
水泳	swimming
水泳選手	swimmer
スイカ	watermelon
数学	math
スカート	skirt
スキー	skiing
スクランブルエッグ	scrambled egg
スズメ	sparrow
20 スタジオ	studio
砂	sand
スピーチ	speech
スポーツマン	athlete
ズボン	pants
スマホ	smart phone
スミレ	violet
生活	life
請求書	bill
成功	success
30 性別	sex
世界	world
接着剤	glue
1000	thousand
選手	player
掃除	cleaning
ソーセージ	sausage
祖父	grandfather
祖父母	grandparents
祖母	grandmother

た行

40 題	title
体育館	gym
大統領	president
台所	kitchen

台風	typhoon
大洋	ocean
太陽	sun
大陸	continent
タカ	hawk
タクシー	taxi
たこ(凧)	kite
ダチョウ	ostrich
卓球	ping-pong
10	table tennis
建物	building
種	seed
楽しさ	fun
食べ物	food
卵	egg
男性	male
	man
地域	area
チェス	chess
20 地球	earth
地図	map
チーズ	cheese
チータ	cheetah
父	father
チーム	team
チューインガム	chewing gum
昼食	lunch
昼食時間	lunchtime
中心	center
30 チューリップ	tulip
チョウ	butterfly
頂上	top
朝食	breakfast
チョコレート	chocolate
地理	geography
月	moon
机	desk
ツバメ	swallow
釣り	fishing
40 釣り糸	line
釣り針	hook
翼	wing
ツル	crane
手	hand
Tシャツ	T-shirt

手紙	letter
手品師	magician
テニス	tennis
テーブル	table
テーマ	theme
天気	weather
展示	display
天文学	astronomy
電話	phone
10	telephone
ドア	door
トウガラシ	red pepper
同級生	classmate
投手	pitcher
動物	animal
時	time
都市	city
年	year
図書館	library
20 トースト	toast
トマト	tomato
友だち	friend
鳥	bird
ドレス	dress

な行

眺め	view
ナス	eggplant
名前	name
ナレーター	narrator
肉	meat
30 日本語	Japanese
ニュース	news
庭	garden
ニワトリ	chicken
ニンジン	carrot
ネコ	cat
年齢	age
ノート	notebook

は行

歯	tooth
パイ	pie
40 パイロット	pilot
ハエ	fly

橋	bridge
場所	place
バス	bus
バスケットボール	basketball
旗	flag
パーティー	party
花	flower
鼻	nose
話	story
10 バナナ	banana
羽	feather
母	mother
ハム	ham
バラ	rose
バレーボール	volleyball
番号	number
ハンバーガー	hamburger
日	day
ピクニック	picnic
20 飛行機	airplane
(飛行機の)便	flight
美術	art
ビタミン	vitamin
左	left
ビデオ	video
人々	people
ヒマワリ	sunflower
秘密	secret
ヒーロー	hero
30 100	hundred
100万	million
日焼け	suntan
病院	hospital
昼	noon
ビン	bottle
ファーストフード	fast-food
ファックス	fax
吹き流し	streamer
服	clothes
40 フクロウ	owl
婦人	lady
ブタ	pig
縁	edge
ふちのある帽子	hat
ふちのない帽子	cap

ブーツ	boot
フットボール	football
ブドウ	grape
船	ship
冬	winter
ブラウス	blouse
プリンタ	printer
プール	pool
ふろ	bath
10 分	minute
平日	weekday
ベッド	bed
ペット	pet
ヘビ	snake
ペンギン	penguin
弁護士	lawyer
棒	stick
宝石	jewelry
ボウリング	bowling
20 星	star
ポスター	poster
ポテトチップ	potato chips
ホテル	hotel
骨	bone
微笑み	smile
ホームページ	homepage
ホームルーム	homeroom
ボール	ball
本	book

ま行

30 マイル	mile
町	town
窓	window
まま母	stepmother
ミカン	mandarin orange
水	water
湖	lake
道	way
ミツバチ	bee
耳	ear
40 娘	daughter
目	eye
めい	niece
メッセージ	message

メートル	meter		指	finger	倫理	ethics
めんどり	hen		ユリ	lily	例	example
文字	letter		洋ナシ	pear	零（0）	zero
モモ	peach		夜の12時	midnight	冷蔵庫	fridge
問題	problem				歴史	history

や行

ら行

ヤギ	goat		ライオン	lion	レストラン	restaurant
野球	baseball		ラジオ	radio	列車	train
野菜	vegetable		ランナー	runner	レモン	lemon
屋台	stand		理科	science	練習問題	exercise
10 山	mountain		陸	land	10 ロボット	robot
夕食	dinner		10 リコーダー	recorder		
夕焼け空	sunset		料理人	cook		
ユニフォーム	uniform		リレー	relay		
			リンゴ	apple		

わ行

ワシ	eagle
笑い	laughter

【著 者】
Colette Morin

高田三夫

佐伯林規江

【表紙デザイン】
デザインスタジオ・maru　丸田薫

【本文デザイン】
京都文英堂 株式会社　反保文江

【音声編集】
シンプティースタジオ　粕谷和弘

BRIDGE to Open Seas

2023 年 10 月 1 日　第 1 刷発行

監修者　　上智大学名誉教授　吉田 研作
　　　　　上智大学教授　　　藤田 保

発行所　京都文英堂株式会社
　　　　〒601-8372　京都市南区吉祥院嶋高町12番地
　　　　（代表）075-661-9960

販　売　株式会社 文英堂

印刷所　株式会社 天理時報社